Toward

Prayers for the

*...[W]hen you pray, go to your inner room, close the
door, and pray to your Father in secret. And your
Father who sees in secret will repay you.*   MATTHEW 6:6

Beverly S. Gordon

Nihil Obstat: Rev. Hilarion Kistner, O.F.M.
Rev. Edward Gratsch

Imprimi Potest: Rev. Jeremy Harrington, O.F.M.
Provincial

Imprimatur: +James H. Garland, V.G.
Archdiocese of Cincinnati
July 31, 1989

The *nihil obstat* and *imprimatur* are a declaration that a book or pamphlet is considered to be free from doctrinal or moral error. It is not implied that those who have granted the *nihil obstat* and *imprimatur* agree with the contents, opinions or statements expressed.

Book design and cover illustration by Julie Lonneman

ISBN 0-86716-129-9

©1990, Beverly S. Gordon

Contents

Introduction

Your life partner has died. Whether it happened suddenly or expectedly does not matter. The one with whom you have long shared so much in marriage is gone; the void is painful, the finality heart-wrenching. You move through the weeks and months feeling as if you are at war. The enemy is grief; you are the sole warrior taking up arms against it. There are days of gaining ground and days of falling back in retreat. All the while you long for victory, for that time when you can accept your mate's death and thereby come to a sense of peace. Others assure you it will happen, but, wounded and battle-weary, you want more than assurance. You want to know how long the journey will be, and you want to know what will get you there.

No one can say how long it will take, for that depends on personality—and your personality print is as unique as your fingerprints. All that is innately yours coupled with everything you have experienced from birth on has molded the self you were on the day you became widowed. Your emotional strengths and weaknesses are not the same as those of a neighbor; your measure of courage differs from that of a relative; your ability to bounce back may not match that of a friend.

The miracle that makes you the unique individual that you are sets your journey toward peace apart from everyone else's, but you are on common ground when it comes to what will get you there.

Work is the key. Work is what will move you toward peace. And you must take up the tools for this work the same as you would for any other task.

Think about it: If you are to cook dinner you must have pots and pans; if you are to paint a fence you must have paint and a brush. For every job at hand, whether it be at home, at the workplace or elsewhere, there are specific tools that make an end result possible.

The tools that will lead you to peace are courage, positive thinking and prayer—courage to set your goal and then to take steps toward it, positive thinking to keep on journeying and prayer to sustain you along the way. And of these tools, prayer is perhaps the most powerful. If you find yourself empty of courage and positive thinking, the force that can bring them back to you is prayer. Prayer is your bridge to God, a limitless source of help and strength.

The prayers in this book were born out of my own struggle to accept the death of my life partner, my own search for peace. They reflect the many moods and seasons of grief. I lovingly share them with you just as I would a pot from my kitchen, a paintbrush from my toolshed or a pencil from the desk where I write. They are yours to draw strength from.

Reflect on the Scripture which gives shape to each prayer. Pray with me, and record your own petitions and thoughts as well. Speak or write whatever comes from your heart, remembering all the while that nothing is ever too complex or too simple for God.

Beverly S. Gordon

The Darkest Hour

For I am the LORD, your God,
who grasp your right hand;
It is I who say to you, "Fear not,
I will help you."   ISAIAH 41:13

Father,
I am in my darkest hour.
My world has collapsed and I am standing in the rubble.
My life partner, the one who was half of me, is dead.
Heartbroken and spent from grief,
I am like a frightened, bewildered refugee,
plodding along an unfamiliar road to I know not where.
With each labored step I wonder how (or even if)
I can pick up the pieces of my shattered life and begin again.

Walk with me, Father.
Move me forward when the road seems too hard to travel.
Set a signpost when I lose my way.
Pick me up when I stumble and fall.

Father, I place myself in your care. Comfort me.

Facing Separation

Father,
I feel widely separated from the one I have lost.
I long for all that was once familiar and dear
to my sight, my hearing, my day-to-day living.

Take this yearning from me, Father.
Strengthen my belief
that the one with whom I shared life on earth
is spiritually close and, therefore, still part of me.
Keep me aware that where there is love
there can be no separation.

Putting Others at Ease

The LORD is close to the brokenhearted;
and those who are crushed in spirit he saves. PSALM 34:19

Father,
some of my friends are uncomfortable around me.
They don't know what to say or do.
Help me to understand their awkwardness,
to put them at ease,
to have the presence of mind to say:
"Just listen to me."
"Just hold my hand."
"Cry with me."
"Share with me how the one we have all lost touched
your life."

Struggling With Weariness

When I called, you answered me;
you built up strength within me. PSALM 138:3

Father,
my body is so spent that I cannot move,
my mind so muddled I cannot think,
my spirit so weary it is but a tiny spark.

Renew my strength,
for there is work I must do.
Give clarity to my mind,
for there are decisions I must make.
Breathe hope into my spirit,
for it is what keeps me going.

Emptying the Closets

I have the strength for everything through him who
empowers me.   PHILIPPIANS 4:13.

Father,
be with me as I clean out the closets.
Grant me courage
when I take clothes I have known so well from their hangers.
Enfold me in love when I take hats and coats from closet
   hooks, sweaters from a shelf.
Strengthen me when I place shoes and slippers in a box.
Comfort me when the tears flow.

Keep me mindful that the task before me
is a necessary part of saying good-bye,
of letting go and beginning again.

Is This a Blessing?

It is good sense in a man to be slow to anger,
and it is his glory to overlook an offense.   PROVERBS 19:11

Father,
I heard it again today: "It was a blessing."
"The suffering is over." "It's for the best."
Someday I may acknowledge the truth of these pat phrases,
but not now—
not at this time of hard good-bye,
not while I am in agony with the pain of loss,
not while I am selfishly wishing
that my mate could still be with me, illness and all.

Father, I need everyone to be tender with me,
but if someone unknowingly offends,
keep me from feeling angry about it.
Soften my heart
and let me look deeper into words spoken
and know they are meant not to hurt
but to comfort and express love.

Asking Why

Trust in the L<small>ORD</small> with all your heart,
on your own intelligence rely not;
In all your ways be mindful of him,
and he will make straight your paths. PROVERBS 3:5, 6

Father,
it is so hard to understand why my loved one had to die.
I pound my fists in demand for an answer.
"Why?" I cry out again and again.

Take this nonsense question from me, Father.
Let me accept that it has no answer
and, therefore, deserves no place in my thoughts.
Show me how to release it,
let it go, put it to rest.
Let me ask, instead,
only those questions that have clear, sure answers:

Is my mate in God's care? Yes.

Is God with me? Yes.

Do I need to know more than that? No.

Coping With Bills and Budgets

[T]he LORD is my strength and my shield.
In him my heart trusts, and I find help....

PSALM 28:7A

Father,
I am worried about money.
Because I am not yet sure how I stand financially,
hospital, funeral and household bills remain unpaid.
I'm scared, Father.
I am used to discussing bills and budgets with my spouse,
making decisions as half of a couple,
not as a single person.

Take this anxiety from me.
Help me to believe in myself
and to trust that all will come right in the end.

Seeking Assurance

In the shadow of your wings I take refuge,
   till harm pass by.   PSALM 57:2B

Father,
in this time of emotional turmoil and profound questioning,
help me to remember
that even when there are earthquakes,
volcanic eruptions and hurricanes,
the sun still rises and sets with a constant sureness
and in time the quaking stops,
the lava ceases to be spewed out
and light breaks through a dark sky.

I need to hold to this truth, Father,
for today it may be all that stands between me and insanity.

Keeping Our Home

Cast all your worries upon him because he cares for you.

1 PETER 5:7

Father,
thank you for my home.
I appreciate the windows that let in light,
the door that welcomes family and friends,
the roof that shelters,
the familiarity that comforts.

Guard me against worrying
about how I shall keep the household going,
how I shall manage alone.
Let me be mindful of the help that comes from you
as I face new challenges, a new way of living.
Keep me from making hurried and perhaps regrettable
    decisions
about moving from my home.

'Get Me Going'

This is the day the LORD has made;
let us be glad and rejoice in it.   PSALM 118:24

Father,
I am tempted to stay in bed—
today, tomorrow, forever.
These blankets are as a suit of armor
against the arrows of the world.
This pillow cradles my weary head
as a mother's arms would cradle her baby.
This room is safe harbor.

Don't let me give way to this temptation, Father.
Get me going.
Plant my feet on the floor
and inspire me to believe that I can do anything
for just one day.

Placing Blame

*Father, if you are willing, take this cup away from me;
still, not my will, but yours be done.*   LUKE 22:42

Father,
I am seeking someone or something to blame
for my mate's death.
Feelings of anger fan out in many directions
and fill me with questions:
Was this death somehow my fault?
Could it have been prevented?
Was our life-style too stressful?
Did the doctors do enough?

Quiet my mind, Father.
Let your love flow through me like a river with swift currents
that will sweep away my senseless quest for an object of
    blame.
Be patient with me while I struggle to accept loss.

The Narrowing Circle of Friends

*Refuse no one the good on which he has a claim
when it is in your power to do it for him.* PROVERBS 3:27

Father,
bless the circle of friends who found time for me
during the first weeks of raw grief.
Some have dropped away now.
Guard me against feeling let down or disappointed about this.
Let me take pride in knowing
that others feel I am ready to stand on my own.
Inspire me to find loving and meaningful ways
to return every kindness done to me.

Sleepless Nights

With his pinions he will cover you,
*   and under his wings you shall take refuge:*
his faithfulness is a buckler and a shield.
You shall not fear the terror of the night
*   nor the arrow that flies by day....*   PSALM 91:4-5

Father,
it is the middle of the night and sleep eludes me.
The space in my bed is too wide,
the silence in my room too deep.
I reach out and touch the cold, empty place
once filled by another's warmth,
and I shudder.
Tears dampen my pillow
and despair is like a nightmare monster waiting to swallow me.

Father, I need to know that you are as close as my very
    breath. Get me through this night.
Quiet the fearful thoughts and worries
that are clamoring through my mind
and making my heart beat fast and hard.
Let me sleep as soundly and carefree as a child—your child.

Leaving Memories Behind

Remember not the events of the past,
the things of long ago consider not.   ISAIAH 43:18

Father,
I need to put memories in their proper perspective
so that they will not fetter and bind me to the past.
When I long for life as it used to be,
open my mind to understanding that,
while the good of another time will always be part of me,
I must strive to live the good of now, this day, this moment.

Let me think of yesterday's happiness as the foundation
upon which I am to build new memories
from new happiness, new joys and new experiences.

17

Nearing Despair

To you I lift up my soul,
O Lord, my God,
in you I trust....   PSALM 25:1-2A

Father,
responsibilities once shared are now solely mine,
and I feel heavily burdened, overwhelmed.
There is so much that is new to me,
so much I must learn,
so much to remember
that I am often driven to tearful despair.

Help me, Father.
Give me the patience and endurance to meet every challenge.
When I am anxious and undone
prompt me to stop whatever I may be doing
and center my thoughts on you.

Making Decisions

I will instruct you and show you the way you should walk;
I will counsel you, keeping my eye on you.   PSALM 32:8

Father,
I have important and difficult decisions to make,
and my confidence is shaky.
I'm afraid of making mistakes.

Guide me, Father.
Let my mind be clear,
my reasoning be logical,
my judgment be sound.
Grant me wisdom as I make choices,
then fill me with a sureness that my choices were right.

Naming Anger

For the LORD gives wisdom,
  from his mouth come knowledge and
  understanding....   PROVERBS 2:6

Father,
I know the one I have lost did not choose to die
and yet I am angry about this death.
It has turned my life upside down and inside out;
this absence brings anguish, loneliness
and a sense of being abandoned.
It hurts to confess these feelings, Father, but I must.
Sustain me as I explore this rage.

Lead me to understand that,
because the future as I designed it is now utterly lost,
I am more disappointed than angry.
Lead me to understand that,
because all that was orderly and certain in my life
is now chaotic and unsure,
I am more frightened than angry.
Lead me to understand that,
because I am powerless to bring my mate back,
I am more frustrated than angry.

Father, open my mind and heart to these truths.
Help me to let go of my misplaced anger
and to spin its threads into spiritual peace.

For My Friends

[B]e filled with the Spirit, giving thanks always
and for everything in the name of our Lord Jesus Christ
to God the Father.   EPHESIANS 5:18B, 20

Father,
thank you for the gift of friends.
Let me be as aware of their needs as they are of mine.

Bless those who grant favors when I need help,
who understand when I need to cry,
who listen when I need to talk,
who give hugs when I need to be hugged.

Clinging to the Promise

You will grieve, but your grief will become joy.   JOHN 16:20B

Father,
in this time of wondering if I shall ever be happy again,
let me think of a rainbow.

For, while my tears may be as a cleansing rain,
they are but half of what I need for that symbol of promise.
Help me to laugh, to feel joyful, to find sun for my rainbow.

Extending Forgiveness

When you stand to pray, forgive anyone against whom you have a grievance, so that your heavenly Father may in turn forgive you your transgressions. MARK 11:25

Father,
I forgive those who exclude me from husband-wife gatherings.
(I know the awkwardness of a fifth wheel.)
I forgive those who respond affirmatively yet coldly
when I ask a favor.
(They have no way of knowing that I will not become a
    nuisance.)
I forgive those who say that I ought to be open
to developing relationships with the opposite sex.
(They think it will bring happiness,
but they are blind to my vulnerability
and my need to take time to grieve.)
I forgive those who judge my tears to be a mark of self-pity.
(They do not know how hard I am working to pick up the
    pieces.)

Keep my heart locked against minding little hurts, Father,
and open to forgiveness, love and understanding.

That Guilty Feeling

Forgive, and you will be forgiven.   LUKE 6:37B

Father,
I feel guilty
because I sometimes lost my temper over insignificant
    things
and spoke angry words to the one who is now gone from me.

Show me how to forgive myself.
Keep me mindful that, because husbands and wives are
    human
and therefore imperfect,
disagreements are natural.
Let me affirm that guilt over things said or left unsaid,
done or left undone, serves no purpose
and is undeserving of even one moment of my thoughts.

The Pain of Loneliness

Set to work, therefore, and the Lord be with you!

1 CHRONICLES 22:16B

Father,
sometimes I am desperately lonely.
I'm used to sharing life with a partner;
I'm used to everyday small talk across the table;
I'm used to taking care of someone and being needed.

Keep my heart open to ways of easing loneliness.
Keep me at work that needs doing.
Lead me to a void I can fill,
activities that will bring joy, satisfaction and fulfillment
to myself and to others.
Keep my mind and hands busy.
Save me from the terrible trap of empty hours in front of the
    TV and from drowning in the waters of self-pity.
Be with me as I make my way through this darkness.

Trusting God

Be firm and steadfast! Do not fear nor be dismayed, for the
LORD, your God, is with you wherever you go.   JOSHUA 1:9

Father,
surely you are everywhere present;
I cannot be separated from you.
Surely you watch over me
in the light of my days and the darkness of my nights.
Surely I am always in your care.

If it were not so, Father,
I would not have survived the past 24 hours.

Being Half a Person

*Since the LORD, your God, has blessed you in all your crops
and in all your undertakings, you shall do naught but make
merry.* DEUTERONOMY 16:15B

Father,
I was so entwined with my life partner
it is as if half of me has died too.
Help me to find a new identity,
to retrieve the part of me that melted into my spouse,
to be the whole person you intend me to be.
Show me the path you want me to take,
the plan you have for my life.

Let me reach out to others without fear of rejection.
Let me try new things without fear of failure.
Let me explore the talents and gifts you have given me.
Grant me the courage to use them
and to stretch my wings as widely as I can.

Rejecting Envy

There is an appointed time for everything, and a time for every affair under the heavens.   ECCLESIASTES 3:1

Father,
forgive the envy that washes over me
whenever I see a husband and wife together.
It's just that I feel left out, alone, set apart, out of step.

Keep me mindful that I've had my turn,
my time of living as half of two.
Take all envy from me, Father,
and let me fill its space
with gratitude for the loving partner I once had
and sincere happiness for those who still have theirs.

'If the World Were Perfect'

Pray without ceasing.   1 THESSALONIANS 5:17

Father,
if the world were perfect there would be no sorrow,
but it isn't, and sometimes I am sad.
If the world were perfect there would be no tears,
but it isn't, and sometimes I weep.
If the world were perfect there would be no loneliness,
but it isn't, and sometimes I am lonely.
If the world were perfect there would be no despair,
but it isn't, and sometimes I am undone.

If the world were perfect I might not believe in prayer,
but it isn't, and I pray.

A Morning Prayer

*At dawn let me hear of your kindness,
for in you I trust.*   PSALM 143:8A

Father,
help me to let go of yesterday for it is gone anyway.
Help me to let go of tomorrow for it is not yet here.
Help me to hold to today for it is what I have.

Let me be hopeful, for hope is what lights the darkness.
Let me be loving, for love is what matters most.

I CORINTHIANS 13. (modern)

If I speak in the tongues of men and of angels,
but have not love, I am only a resounding
gong or a clanging cymbal. If I have the gift
prophecy and can Fathom all mysteries and
knowledge, and if I have a Faith that can mov
mountains, but have not love, I am nothing. If
give all I possess to the poor and surrender my
body to the Flames, but have not love, I gain noth
Love is patient, love is kind. It does not envy, it c
not boast, it is not proud. It is not rude, it is not se
seeking, it is not easily angered, it keeps no record c
wrongs. Love does not delight in evil but rejoi
with the truth. It always protects, always tru
always hopes, always perseveres.
Love never Fails. But where there are prophecis
they will cease, where there are tongues, they wi
be stilled, where there is knowledge, it will pa
away. For we know in part and we prophesy
part but when perfection comes, the imperfec
disappears. When I was a child, I talked
a child, I thought like a child, I reasoned
a child. When I became a man, I put chi
ways behind me. Now we see but a poor
reflection as in a mirror, then we shall s

A Thanksgiving Day Prayer

I will praise the name of God in song,
and I will glorify him with thanksgiving....   PSALM 69:31A

Father,
grant me courage as I come to this first Thanksgiving
without the person I am used to seeing across the table.
Sustain me
when memories of Thanksgivings past bring a rush of sadness.
Fill me with an awareness of your love,
your care and your bountiful blessings.

Thank you for all the Thanksgivings I shared with my
    loved one.
Thank you for those who hold me in their thoughts and prayers.
Thank you for the love
that will be as much a part of today's dinner as the turkey.
Bless the hands that will prepare the food
and the hearts that invited me to share it.

Face to face. Now I know in part, then I
shall know Fully, even as I am Fully
known. And now these three remain,
Faith, hope and love. But the greatest
of these is love.

31

A Christmas Prayer

Glory to God in the highest
and on earth peace to those on whom
his favor rests.   LUKE 2:14

Father,
this is my first Christmas without the one
with whom I have for so long shared holiday joy.
The pain is deep, Father.
Keep me from dwelling on the past.
Turn my thoughts instead to the true meaning of this holy
season.

Let me look at the night sky
and think of the star that proclaimed the birth of Jesus.
Let me hear carols
and think of ancient tidings of great joy.
Let me give gifts
and think of the wise men who brought theirs to the
newborn King.
Let me read the Christmas story
and think of love and peace.
Let me light a Christmas candle
as a beacon of hope for the world and for myself.

A Wedding Anniversary Prayer

*Blessed be the God and Father of our Lord Jesus Christ, the
Father of compassion and God of all encouragement, who
encourages us in our every affliction....*   2 CORINTHIANS 1:3-4A

Father,
today is my wedding anniversary.
My thoughts are of that treasured day
when I exchanged vows with the one who would share
    my life.
We were filled with dreams, hopes and plans.
How easily we spoke the phrase,
"Till death us do part."
But now that a parting has come, Father,
the very thought of those words tightens my throat.

Keep me from bitterness.
Keep me from self-pity.
Let me be grateful for falling in love
and for the marriage that came from that.
Let me rejoice in memories of all that was shared
in love, devotion and fidelity.

Prayer for All the Widowed

The LORD be with all of you.   2 THESSALONIANS 3:16B

Father,
let me be a prayer channel through which your loving care
will flow to others who have lost a spouse.

I pray for those with young children.
Strengthen them
as they face the challenge of heading a household.
Guide them
as they try to be both mother and father.

I pray for those with grown children.
Keep them from using their sons and daughters as
    leaning posts
and from weaving themselves too tightly
into the lives of their offspring.

I pray for those who are elderly.
Let them be thankful for the years they had with their mate.
Let them hold only the sweetest memories of a long-shared
    life.
Guard their health and surround them
with supportive family and friends.

I pray for those who try to escape grief's pain
in alcohol or drugs.
Let them recognize that such things are traps,
not escape hatches.
Grant them the wisdom and courage to seek help.

I pray for those who,
out of loneliness and desperation,
rashly develop relationships with the opposite sex.
Let them be cautious.
Make them aware of their vulnerability.

In Thanksgiving for Prayer

Hear, O God, my cry;
listen to my prayer.
From the earth's end I call to you
as my heart grows faint.
You will set me high on a rock; you will
give me rest....   PSALM 61:2-3

Father,
thank you for prayer,
the lantern that lights my way through the darkness.
I come to you in quietness
and with assurance that you hear me.
I listen to the still small voice within
and accept your answer to my prayer,
even when it may not be as I wanted it to be.
I give thanks for your guidance, your love, your blessings.
I stand firm in my belief
that you will provide for my every need.